LANTERN PUZZLE

THE BERKSHIRE PRIZE
The Tupelo Press First/Second Book Award

Jennifer Michael Hecht, *The Last Ancient World*
Selected by Janet Holmes

Aimee Nezhukumatathil, *Miracle Fruit*
Selected by Gregory Orr

Bill Van Every, *Devoted Creatures*
Selected by Thomas Lux

David Petruzelli, *Everyone Coming Toward You*
Selected by Campbell McGrath

Lillias Bever, *Bellini in Istanbul*
Selected by Michael Collier

Dwaine Rieves, *When the Eye Forms*
Selected by Carolyn Forché

Kristin Bock, *Cloisters*
Selected by David St. John

Jennifer Militello, *Flinch of Song*
Selected by Carol Ann Davis and Jeffrey Levine

Megan Snyder-Camp, *The Forest of Sure Things*
Selected by Carol Ann Davis and Jeffrey Levine

Daniel Khalastchi, *Manoleria*
Selected by Carol Ann Davis and Jeffrey Levine

Mary Molinary, *Mary & the Giant Mechanism*
Selected by Carol Ann Davis and Jeffrey Levine

Ye Chun, *Lantern Puzzle*
Judge's Prize, selected by D. A. Powell

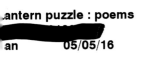
YE CHUN

叶春

LANTERN PUZZLE

T|P

Tupelo Press
North Adams, Massachusetts

Library of Congress Cataloging-in-Publication Data
Chun, Ye.
[Poems. Selections]
Lantern puzzle : poems / Ye Chun.
pages ; cm
ISBN 978-1-936797-53-0 (pbk. : alk. paper)
I. Title.
PS3625.E14A6 2015
811'.6--dc23
2014047377

Cover and text designed by Josef Beery.
Type composition in Chaparral, a humanist interpretation of a slab serif font created
by Carol Twombly for Adobe at the close of the twentieth century. Titles set in
Officina Sans designed for ITC by Erik Spiekermann during the same era.

Cover art: "S. A. Andrée's Ice Balloon" (2012), detail of a work in oil paint and pencil
by Elizabeth Preston Schoyer (http://elizabethpschoyer.com/). Used with permission.
Artist's note: In 1897, Swedish engineer S. A. Andrée set out to show that a hydrogen
balloon could be used to reach places otherwise inaccessible. To prevent its puncture
and protect it from the wind, he constructed a house around a balloon, with walls
covered in heavy felt and windows made of gelatin. The walls of the house were
designed to fall away as the balloon lifted off, headed for the North Pole.

First paperback edition: March 2015.

Tupelo Press
P.O. Box 1767, North Adams, Massachusetts 01247
Telephone: (413) 664–9611 / editor@tupelopress.org / www.tupelopress.org

Tupelo Press is an award-winning independent literary press that publishes fine
fiction, nonfiction, and poetry in books that are a joy to hold as well as read.
Tupelo Press is a registered 501(c)(3) nonprofit organization, and we rely on public
support to carry out our mission of publishing extraordinary work that may be
outside the realm of the large commercial publishers.
Financial donations are welcome and are tax deductible.

for Shawn

CONTENTS

MAP

AMULET

ALMANAC

WINDOW

MAP

1. Niujie, Beijing

When the earth shakes, hunching grandma
picks me up, cousin's uneven leg shadow-puppets
the window. The sky lowers like father's raincoat
till the old lady carried out by her son
drums on his head: *Let me die at home, let me die.*
We live in a tent, eat government bread
and play on a monkey-hill. The world stays
a cotton ball in big sister's bleeding nose.
Worms swim in my belly; warm air rubs my soles.

Draw a spider web
with small cocoons
Draw one cocoon
of hymenoptera
one of polyp
of cynodont
one with a man inside
the man with a bird
in his belly
(its singing is its gyration)
with a bomb in his head
(its ticking its nutrition)

2. Gushui, Luoyang

Green tea for night, red for day.
The sun presses my temples as my father's high bike
draws another street to the east.
The sparrow I caught with a basket, twig, rope and wheat
shoots arrows at me with a slant eye.
A tadpole between my sole and sandal.
I've learned to hold a brush tight
so the teacher behind my back can't snatch it.
The ink splashes on my stiff white shirt.

White goat's hair
black rabbit's hair
yellow weasel's hair
Master Fu Shan
says: *better ugly*
than charming
better broken
than sleek
better natural
than arranged
This is a brush
or a cut-off finger
That is a character
or a pried-out eye

3. Zhongzhou, Luoyang

The district languishes between brown and purple.
All the apartment buildings look the same.
I need to lie down, call out
your name to one of the black-barred
windows. In the most crowded market,
my classmate is selling embroidered pillowcases and lingerie.
If you appear, I'll make you look at me balancing
the sick little invisible animal
on my head. I love the sweet numbness of dusk —
we glow before vanishing.

Lay out the grid
of roads and wards:
Align the northern part
of the western wall
the middle stretch
of the eastern wall
and a road that comes
in Gate VII
turns west
and heads south
nearly reaching
the course of the Luo
Align the other roads
the southern part
of the western wall
most of the northern stretch
and the surviving part
at the southern end
of the eastern wall

4. Shenzhen

Streetlamps imitate stars.
Stains on a hotel ceiling imitate mountains, boats and ruins.
. . . *either do great good or great evil*,
the journalist, 23, says. We walk
along the low brick wall into a park. A palm tree
stops us and deepens the ocher of our faces.
A stone bridge shapes an ellipse with its shadow.
We don't have much to do so we press each other's body.
Is a compass a moon bringing a finger to its lips?

A mosquito net
with a crimson mosquito
A roach crawls beneath the net
onto her right leg
My leg feels odd
she says
It's broken
her algebra teacher says
It's broken
her editor-in-chief says
It's broken
the legless beggar says
It's broken
the manager of Human Resources says
It's broken
her snoring lover says
On the wall a map
of cherries and water paths

5. Lhasa

Seeds tier in a pomegranate.
Sweat beads convex-mirror corners of a night.
You pick up a piece of coal from roadside,
wrap it in a blue and green checked handkerchief
and give it to me: *What makes you feel warm?*
In the Himalayas, a snow leopard
spins gold in early morning. I tie a prayer flag
to a balloon and let go. Its little feet step through clouds
and rain falls on the white stupas, the hind-scalps
of prostrating pilgrims who say: *om mani padme hum, om
mani padme hum, om mani padme hum* . . .

Buddhakapala
(Skullcup of Buddha)
presides over
twenty-five deities
two hands
holding his consort
(Citrasena)
four hands
his skullcup
chopper
ceremonial staff
and drum
In the dancer's pose
(ardhaparyanka)
he stands on a corpse
supported by a lotus

6. Kansas City

Cars pass, each with a heart
bearing the weight of its metal.
My second-hand coat and I carry each other
not knowing who sent me on the road,
who evaporated in its arms. We walk
after orange sinks to rust. My coat's old companions
follow us, their eyes
fixed on my back. I don't want to talk —
In my chest, dirt fattened by memory
waits for seeds.

Avoid windows
A mattress
Avoid windows
A bathtub
Cover your head
A rhombus head
With hands
Hands in stones
Follow the drill
Get out
Drive a right angle
Lie flat
Avoid windows
Get under the pews
The train is coming

7. Olympia, Washington

The Pacific Ocean shovels coals in the distance.
My drunk friends drop pebbles at me as I lie
on the couch losing water. *Be happy, be happy, be happy.*
I'm trying to see spring sprout, mountain that smells like green apple,
grass younger than I, to see the pink sweater
I wore when the sun sprinkled pink dust and I practiced
xiang gong to make my body fragrant,
not the speeding lines of the steel tunnel,
a hand gridding its fingers on my ribs.
I'm trying to breathe, to reach water or an address.

In the white house
with white windows
who spends the night?
The dead say: *don't*
talk so loud
I can hear you
even before the words
In the woods
flies a bird
whose feathers
bear every color
in the world
You've seen it
You've gathered
every name of it
in your throat

8. Aransas Pass, Texas

Your hair veins the setting sun. Love slashes
in my body. If the world is a crystal glass
and the dolphin its humming, why so much red?
Shall we close our eyes and walk
into the water of red swords? Shall we hold
a green flame between our eyes to see,
burn our hands into each other's back
to push, to reach? Shall we say
loneliness as the dolphin curves its echo
above the water and the water drinks us?

This mantle
dazzles the eye
with train tracks
water wakes
game boards
letters
numbers
tortoise shells
and men in hunting
sports
business
war
A shaman's cloth
A priest's vest
A royal garment
An offering
Such warmth
within the body

9. Guangzhou

From the bus I see you lean against a smog-dyed building,
your body shrunken, bare gums grinding, eyes darting as people
in their own restlessness float by. If only I could lead you,
hold onto the next morning and hold you
with the other hand, if only I knew the safe land —
the world terrifies me too, the world that is no
stranger than before. Tonight my nine-year-old niece wonders
if the sun will eat the earth. Will the moon
shake off the dust and shine for us.

See the bud
and its masks—
Typhoon, bug
mushroom bark . . .
How many
shades of black
can you see
How many
mildew lines
were once rain
The cat
they are eating
has one big eye
one small
A heart waits
in a doorway
and expands

AMULET

Amulet from a River-Country

You float in my palm, clay-cool —

a water buffalo with blue eyes
a blue fish on its back
straw ties them as river ties land

The soil is loam yellow
Cottages have grown tiny

In this city, all birds save sparrows have fled
A flower girl's bike rides on shadows

In this city, I can't tell what my body tells me —
a half moon or a folded road-sign
two parking lines or an empty ladder

To love or to leave

I'll follow you awhile
crossing the river on a goatskin raft

Butterfly, Pinched and Pinned

back on back
wing on wing

fei.

pebbles on wings
eyes in eyes
arid moons

fei.

below the little perils
above a small love

fei.

inside every window
you are a window

fei. fei. fei.

abyssal creek
carrying ice
darker colors
under ice

a small death

fei.

Photo of My Father at Eleven

Your father has decided to find you
in the year after the war. He, an officer,

remarried. You and your sisters and mother
feed on banana and church congee.

Your mother's sorrow hangs like a wisteria bud;
she leans her head in the north-facing room.

Father, I have your eyes and mouth.
I wore the same Youth Pioneer band on my neck,

its knot also bigger than my throat.
In a few years you will find the words

to speak to your father. But for now,
lost in bricks and gray asphalt,

let us hold hands and hum together.

The Prison at Cherry Hill

(from the Prison series by photographer James Casebere)

No sound of breaking. No water dripping through stones.

White walls reach toward sleeping bodies of jailer and prisoner.
White, like a lone child's whistle rising from the field.
Sorrow is already stored for him.

The moon clutches every water. How the hand wishes to be used for harvest.

Roses

At night I'm small,
soft, and ready
to be glowed upon.

You are the lanterns
of a heart that loves,
loves.

You are twelve little
burning moons.

Then my head
turns river-colored,
weighed down
by the footprints of birds.

I'm in the sun.
You, blood-bright.

How can you cross
all this white
between us?

Amulet Resembling My Stomach

(How to carry)

Rule 1:   what can
              or cannot be carried on
              a shelf of air

Rule 2:   whether you are one or one of the last

Rule 3:   carry it in a tube of arrows
              label it what's soft and sullen

Rule 4:   the soft should be bronzed
              the sullen chiseled
              so that the wandering can see the wanderer

Rule 5:   carry it on an x-ray belt
              so that what's red is not what's burning
              so that what's ruffled is

Rule 6:   not because you refuse
              will you not be able to fly

Rule 7:   carry it beneath a heart of hammer

Coal

My stomach says it's a fist, a soft fist, likes to sleep, to be stroked,
wants to be a lotus and in the lotus a pearl:

> *I've rubbed my forehead clean and thin.*
> > *I've reached for bones in a mirror.*
> *I've entered the water, swan-trodden.*
> > *I've entered the water, moon-filled.*

Says it's purpler than night, than fearful hearts in night woods,
than buried plants waiting to be coal:

> *I've bowed to my mother.*
> > *I've carried twilight clouds.*
> *I've sealed my body to the earth*
> > *and listened to what's turning.*

Amulet from the Andes

A shell without ocean

An animal all bone

A secret that can't be shared
hardened into a stone bag

Can you say: *I'll give you*
dimness and riches
treasures of a soiled palace

Can you say: *Because of you*
those invisible wings

in the sky   those invisible beds

those parasols and straw-shoes

You say: Curl your body in me
I'll wrap you with un-uttering

I say: Clouds rumble along my house
Bird-calls nail my ceiling

Peachwood Pendant

The shadowy one left under the peach tree
is light enough for the blossoms to float through.

I always arrive earlier and leave earlier.

It is said in the ocean grows a peach tree;
between its branches, the door of ghosts.

My grandmothers — one hunching, one pale
as a distant bird — stand at either side of the door.

I am still the hurrying one, unable
to carry those not loved enough.

Only in my chest is space
dark enough for a peach tree to bloom.

Photo of My Mother at Twenty-Five

The star on your cotton hat is gray.
Mother, what do you see?

Has my pen bent deep enough
for me to remember?

Daughter of the youngest widow,
the palest in the village.

Your face is so calm.
Your heart digs behind the army coat.

You carried and carried me
through the winter.

The star on your cotton hat says:
I shine! I shine!

It's spring again.
Look at those yellow flowers.

I feel so light,
slipping from your body.

ALMANAC

In the First Moon

What's sharp has been put away
so luck is safe in its roundness.

What's harvested bears us to the table
of childhood. We heat a pot of wine.

A loneliness we want to touch.
Wait, let's stay a little longer.

Dragon Head Rising

It's been so dry;
we follow a river before daybreak.

For what shall we pray

when the sky is without dragons,
land without fields?

Our loved ones are clouds
we see from so far.

Gold beans will flower;
wind will open.

For what shall we pray?

A feather on the heart?
A moon on the mountain?

A moon on the mountain.

March

A stupa of pear blossoms covers a sheep's shorn body.

Lighter leaves between leaves:
A newly hatched spider lengthens its silk with the wind.

Soon its first web, its translucent insects.

I've been looking for three ways
to say a sentence. To make the white ribbon stand

when the eye is a drop of resin —

The Day of Cold Food

Twenty-six hundred years ago, Jie Zitui cut
a slice of flesh from his leg
to feed the starving Prince Chong'er.

Under the moon, the meat
looked like a piece of turquoise.

Fireflies bulbed off and on.
A skyful of stars waited.

My grandfather left for the war
just after his wedding, only saw
my grandmother's face at seventeen.

A twirl of air once was a village
with salt and piglets.

Light like cobwebs, like vines.

Children in white shirts place paper flowers
on the tomb of the martyrs —

White flowers hang on bones, rustling.

The Day of Qu Yuan Drowning

(Qu Yuan, 332–296 BCE, a court minister, diplomat, and the first known Chinese poet, drowned himself after seven years in exile.)

1.

They're dotting eyes on the dragon boats.
They're sniffing orchid pouches and balancing raw eggs.

Among blue fish and red cobbles, have you found the word
you'll say again and again till the water turns to cloud?

2.

My father teaches me to make zongzi,
wrapping rice, date-hearted, in a bamboo leaf.

3.

The grasses by the river cast shadows on one another.
Your long sleeves are filled with antitheses.
Your one hundred and seventy questions crowd the water.

The clean-nailed diviner shakes out bamboo slips;
you see them fall.

Is that enough?
Or freckles on an elder's hand, a star chart
on the fifth day of the fifth moon, gods in twilight?

4.

I've been beautiful for you.

The bamboo slips are the last things my eyes made.

I've loved myself. I'm no longer hungry.

5.

We throw zongzi in the river so that fish won't eat you,

our loved one.

6.

The river wraps you tight.

Your stomach calls *pure, pure*.

Rain Season

Sometimes I hear swords clashing

In a moldy tea-house
two women stretch their necks
talk about omens and fate

Waterweeds shock up their backs

———

Every summer, children in Bilong Village
sit on the hilltop
bodies covered by rainwater

The village sinks like a pebble

Parents have burned incense in the dragon temple
offered wine
their hearts big and soft

In the children's eyes
the color of crops
is a little grayer than the river
the river a little grayer than the sky

———

At night silence
covers everyone

I've run through alleys

Passing a stone gate
I see my father
buying vegetables
from a street vendor

His high bike
stands behind him

Father will take me home

The Seventh Moon is for the Hungry Ghosts

At night the earth has no owner.

On every doorstep, bowls of rice and sweetmeats.

Come back, my hungry one,
from where food turns into fire.

We burn the hell-money higher
and the paper houses.

We set lanterns on water.

Are you the slim one in the doorway,
the shoeless, eyeless one?

Let me lend you my nervous stomach,
my mouth of knots.

Three Moons Make a Season

I used to stand before lantern puzzles.

Now my window is too low for the moon,
my window with the sound of trains.

Cinnamon grove pressed on mooncakes

and pomelo cut in twelve
are for people in the yellow space.

In my stomach
migrant workers hammer and saw;

the houses they build remain empty.

Chrysanthemum is Prettiest in the Ninth Moon

The window has moved.
My gray-haired elders are still there,
counting chrysanthemum petals in the sun,
each petal a sad shoe.

The Day of Winter Clothes

Put on these paper ashes, my ancestor,

the five-colored paper I've brought for you
and burned. Cold weather is falling.

Once fever lit up your forehead.
Once the sun knocked and knocked,

flooding the hall. How you've danced

with no light except your stillness,
no darkness except your eyes.

Ancestor, your teeth fall into the night
like little bronze mirrors.

My forehead has no stone door. Wind enters:
The ash coat trembles for you.

Light Snow

waterdrops in the body
grow light, down

through nest vines
bamboo grove

the porous heart
not knowing

not looking for
blood or pebble

the membrane sky
heart-stitched, heart-still

Off Year

I've swept spiders off the walls
and pasted Red Children on the window.

I've watched the ghosts coming back
in their long gowns of grief.

They squeeze my fingertips till dark
flows out.

Don't speak ill of me, Kitchen God,
when you meet Jade Emperor.

WINDOW

The moon a leaf-boat
already belongs to the far

The heart on the windowsill
tells itself it loves
the ink-tree
that thinks of no vines
no *I'll forget*

and the five ink-birds pulsing away
leaving clouds of peach flowers

How long does it take to rise
from the mat woven
with long roads and hunger

to travel the length of
understand understand

And the harbor comes tiding
from heart to toe-tips

Behind me is a scene not to be reassembled —

a few lightbulbs,
a few eyes diluted by light,
a few hands pointing at the sky

and feet maybe pale and humid as mine.
A dog barks
as if its heart is being tossed out bit by bit.

Fog flies by, cold feathers, lifting me up.
The stone road crowded with gold snakes and spiders.

The Luoyang Poem

1.

Gray streets and dim staircases.

We slid down the banister:

often one of us,
in dream or memory, fell.

2.

I fell ill
or feigned illness
to put those heavy school buildings
behind me.

I rode my bike
breaking through smoke thicker than hair.

3.

New dynasty burned houses of the old.
Red Guards burned 55,884 rolls of sutras at the White Horse Temple.
Twenty factories burned the sky blind.
Families of the dead burned paper horses.
Crematoria burned the dead.
My father burned another fall's leaves.
I burned my diary.

Summer, dusk clouds filled up the sky,
reddening our faces.
We fluttered cattail fans
as if to burn ourselves faster.

4.
Luoyang, your cross
was formed by the highest smokestack
and the train blocking our way.

O those eyes on the train
looked as if they'd seen through
all that is far away.

5.
Our parents were sent here
to build a new nation.
At home they speak hometown dialect,
cook hometown food.

When Du Fu lived here,
all the males in the city
were sent to fight along the borders.

We cursed and spit on the speckled roads.

6.
Before Jian River dried,
my father took me fishing,

and I found my own land of peach trees
before the woods were leveled
and the dirt covered by concrete.

They caught my friend
cheating on an exam and expelled her.
Her sister told me she left the city.

I still see, moments before nightfall,
a velvet sky above the river,
cranes fly over, turn into fairies
and wash their hair in the darkening water.

In my dreams, my friend returns
in different faces just like in different cities
I often see peach flowers.

7.
That winter, a boy
came riding beside me,
my big coat a dark corner.

We rode past the sweet potato vendor and his stove;
they stood in every winter
like a small lighthouse.

We rode past Chairman Mao
in front of the Mining Machinery Factory,
his marble arm waving at us.

Black flags blew above our heads.

We rode toward the huge
suddenly blooming setting sun.

The Guangzhou Poem

The Henan girl who sells her body
waits by the Pearl River.

Each old man coming out of the dark
reminds her of her father.

She looks into the grimy water. A breeze
glides by, her shoulders start to glisten.

———

My forehead is flat as a coin.

The beggar boy folds his hand under my rib.
We're connected awhile and are poorer.

A mad woman cries *my son my son*.
The city lights up,
each head a torch so that she may see.

———

The black swans flap their clipped wings
in the synthetic lake at the Clifford Estate.

Only after dark will the hungry birds calm down,
play the little statues of sadness.

I want to see them die,
their long, self-pitying necks twisted back.

———

On rainy nights, ropes of light
lower the city
down to the bottom of water.

In the bus window I find my face,
unsure whether it is rising or falling.

Today they cut the tree in front of my window

>	you, so gentle, i've wanted
>	to move my hand along you.

>	your birds grow bigger,
>	sit on my windowsill.

>	we'll lament together:
>	stars pass through you.

A mansion of many rooms

The moon is drawn toward her grasses,
reddening. What does she suffer?
Driving into the city, among ten thousand lights,
we no longer see her.

———

Grandma Bea still takes the pills, the little buttons
that remind the body to open and close.
At night, she boards an airplane which looks like a bird burning.
The terminal is underwater.

———

The sky will soon be dark.
Someone is picking hair from the carpet.
A lamp in the window shines for a light rain.

When I can't sleep, the top of my head
sinks until it holds rain.

My window teaches me
to breathe slowly:

You leave two rows of pauses
wherever you go.

My window falls and rises
like the water within my body.

Why we part at sunset

1. Bedside with grandmother

Time is a rope
I can't slide down. This life —
at such a height
I see my breath fall.

2. Deskmate, Ever-red Elementary

Do you remember they forced us to play couple?
Your little cock looked strange.
I've never raised silkworms again —
those tiny black seeds, how I wanted to crush them.

3. Hong Hui Hospital

A small coffin drifts on a river.
The mother's coffin hurries after it.
They will never meet.
In this dark coat I'll wait a little longer.

4. *A stranger's finger on my palm, warmly*

My eyes grow distant —
her wrinkles like hills in twilight.
You're a spring ox, she says.
Green grass covers the land.

Those landscapes do not wait, they sit in their shadows.

My window sits, a clear heart,
exchanging frost for frost, promise for promise
with what's cooling, blooming in wind:

Once I held a map which was empty.
Only at night the roads emerged.

Destinations tingling: dew on a leaf.

Smallest moon, fingertip,
two curves —

one floats on everything becoming tender,

one a breath leaving,
taking nothing, not even a murmur.

ACKNOWLEDGMENTS

I am grateful to the editors of the following journals, where poems from this book first appeared:

American Poetry Review:
"The Day of Winter Clothes"

"Arts & Academe," the online blog of *The Chronicle of High Education*:
"Aransas Pass," "Guangzhou," and "Gushui, Luoyang," from the sequence "Map"

The Bitter Oleander:
"Amulet from a River Country," "The Guangzhou Poem," "In the First Moon," "A Mansion of Many Rooms," "Peachwood Pendant," "Photo of My Mother at Twenty-Five," "The Prison at Cherry Hill," "Rain Season," "Roses," "The Seventh Moon is for the Hungry Ghosts," and "Three Moons Make a Season"

Cerise Press:
"The Day of Qu Yuan Drowning" and "March"

Four Way Review:
"Lhasa," "Niujie, Bejing," "Shenzhen," "Olympia, Washington," and "Zhongzhou, Luoyang," from the sequence "Map"

Indiana Review:
"Remember Luoyang"

Poetry International:
"The Day of Cold Food" and "Why We Part at Sunset"

Salamander:
"Kansas City," from the sequence "Map"

Spacecraftprojects (http://spacecraftproject.wordpress.com):
"Behind me is a scene not to be reassembled," "Butterfly, Pinched
and Pinned," "Dragon Head Rising," "Smallest moon . . .," "Those
landscapes . . .," "Today they . . .," and "When I can't . . ."

Verse Daily:
"The Day of Qu Yuan Drowning"

"Amulet from the Andes" and "Chrysanthemum is Prettiest in the
Ninth Moon" were included in the anthology *Poetic Voices Without
Borders 2*, edited by Robert L. Giron (Gival Press, 2009).

I am grateful to the following people for their advice, inspiration,
and encouragement: Rita Dove, Lisa Russ Spaar, Charles Wright,
Gregory Orr, Paul B. Roth, Elizabeth Schoyer, Shawn Flanagan,
Gillian Parrish, Scott Cairns, and Carolyn Forché. Many thanks to
the University of Virginia's MFA program for its generous support.
Thanks also to Jim Schley for his invaluable editorial assistance.

I am also deeply grateful to D. A. Powell for selecting the work.

Other books from Tupelo Press